CURSIVE
Handwriting Workbook For Kids 8-12

Learn Cursive Writing & Practice Penmanship Book
for Kids age 8-12
Alphabet, Sentences, Riddles, Jokes

Thank You!

Thank you for your purchase.
We have loved creating this book
and we hope your kids get hours of fun and learning
with cursive handwriting practice.

We value your feedback and opinion
as it assists with our next creation.
You also help other buyers - just like you,
make the right decision.

INTRODUCTION

Welcome to the enchanting world of cursive handwriting!
In this workbook, you'll learn the art of creating flowing and beautiful letters that make writing a delightful adventure. Whether you're drawing your name, composing a story, or jotting down notes, cursive handwriting adds a touch of magic to your words.

Beyond its charm, cursive writing has incredible benefits. It enhances your memory, sparks creativity, and boosts your overall academic skills. So get ready to embark on an exciting journey of learning and fun!

Throughout this workbook, we'll start with the basics, mastering each cursive letter step by step. As you progress, you'll join letters together to form words and sentences, crafting your unique style.

Parents and teachers, your encouragement and support are essential for success. Join your young learners on this adventure, and watch their confidence soar!
Grab your pen, embrace the magic, and let's begin our cursive handwriting quest!

with excitement and warmth,
Bob Weedman

GETTING STARTED

Prepare for the cursive handwriting adventure with these simple steps:

- **Materials**: Grab pencils with a comfortable grip, soft erasers, and our special practice sheets with helpful guidelines.

- **Posture**: Sit up straight, feet flat on the floor, and forearms resting gently on the table.

- **Magical Tip**: Angle your paper slightly to the left (for right-handed) or right (for left-handed) to make cursive writing even more enjoyable.

Now, let the magic of cursive handwriting begin! Turn the page and start creating beautiful letters.

THIS BOOK BELONGS TO

_____

Name

Grade

Table Of Contents

08	ALPHABET
38	LETTERS JOINS
52	WORDS
79	RIDDLES & JOKES

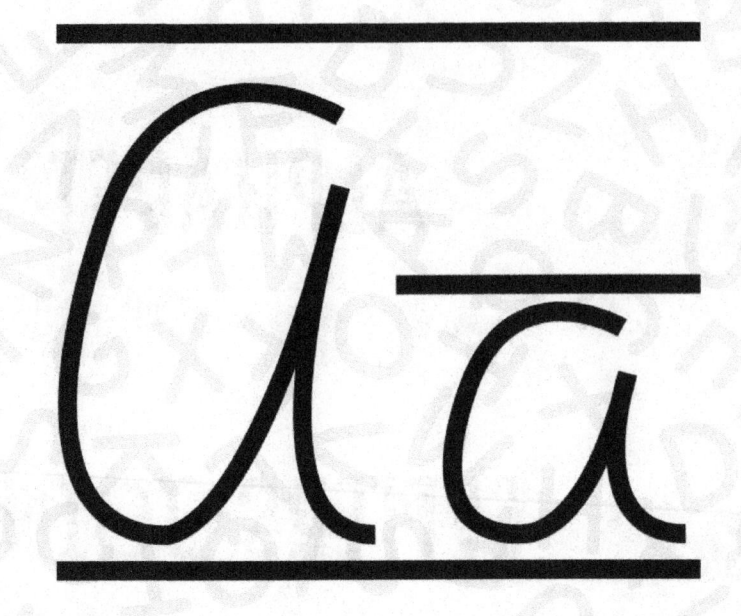

CURSIVE ALPHABET
WORK SHEET

CAPITAL LETTERS IN CURSIVE

A B C D E F G

H I J K L M N

O P Q R S T U

V W X Y Z

NOTE: Trace over the dotted letters on the following pages then try writing the letters on your own in the blank space areas.

There are additional blank lined pages at the end of this workbook for more practice time.

lowercase letters in cursive

a b c d e f g h

i j k l m n o

p q r s t u v

w x y z

A B C D E F G H I J K L M N O P Q R S T U V W X Y Z

A B C D E F G H I J K L M N O P Q R S T U V W X Y Z

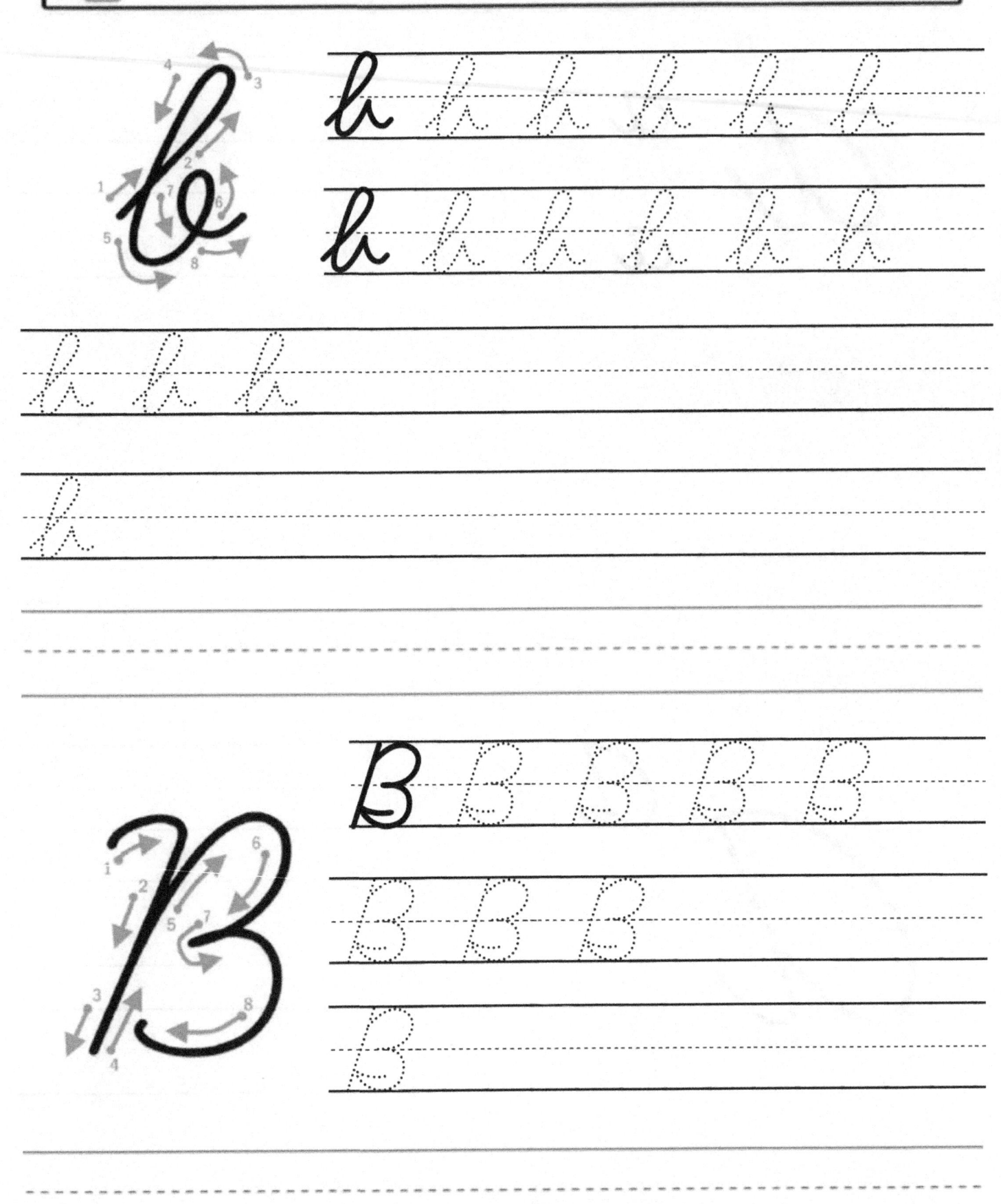

A B C D E F G H I J K L M N O P Q R S T U V W X Y Z

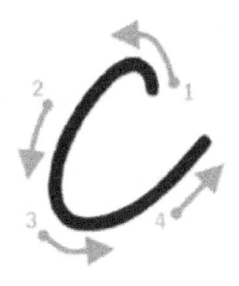

13

A B C **D** E F G H I J K L M N O P Q R S T U V W X Y Z

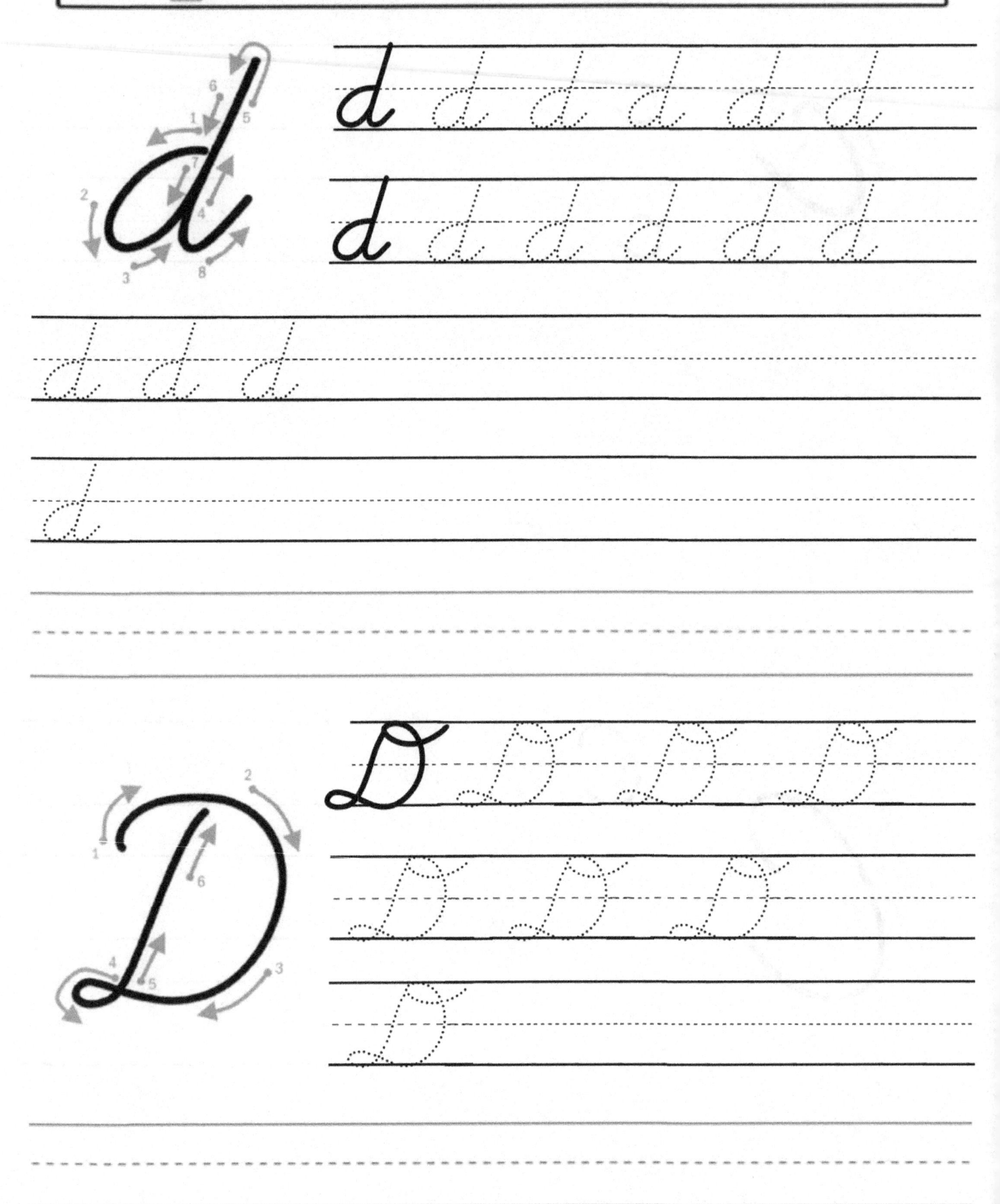

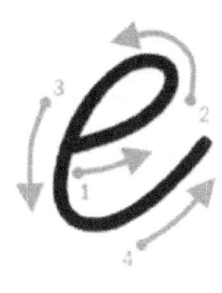

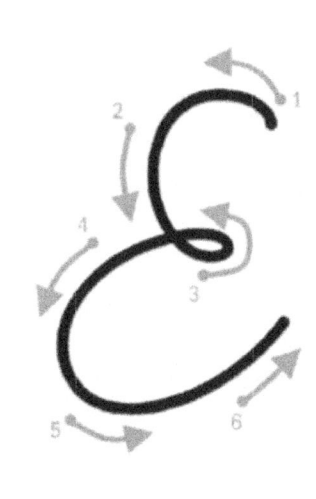

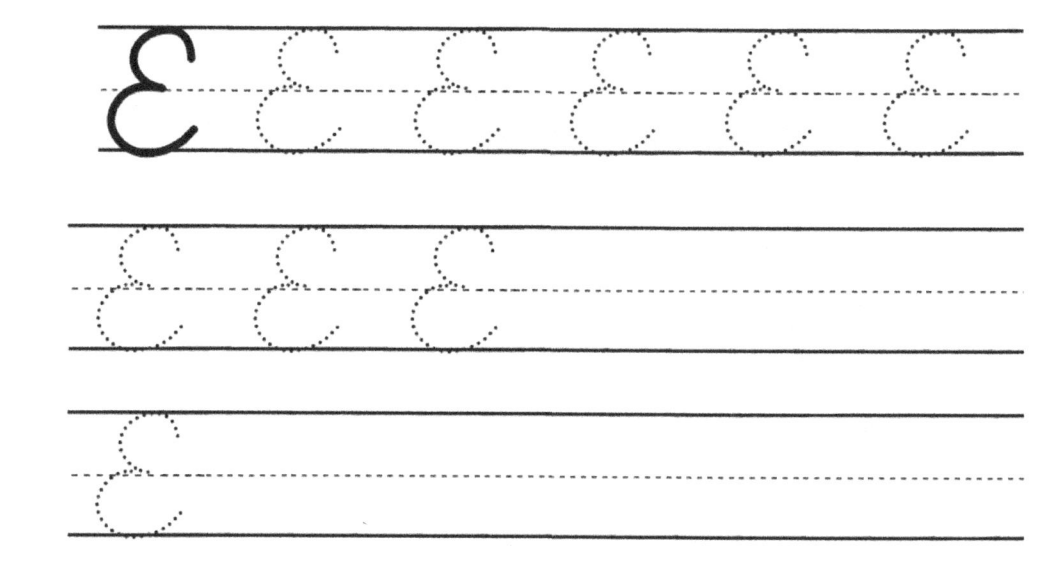

A B C D E F G H I J K L M N O P Q R S T U V W X Y Z

A B C D E F G H I J K L M N O P Q R S T U V W X Y Z

16

A B C D E F G H I J K L M N O P Q R S T U V W X Y Z

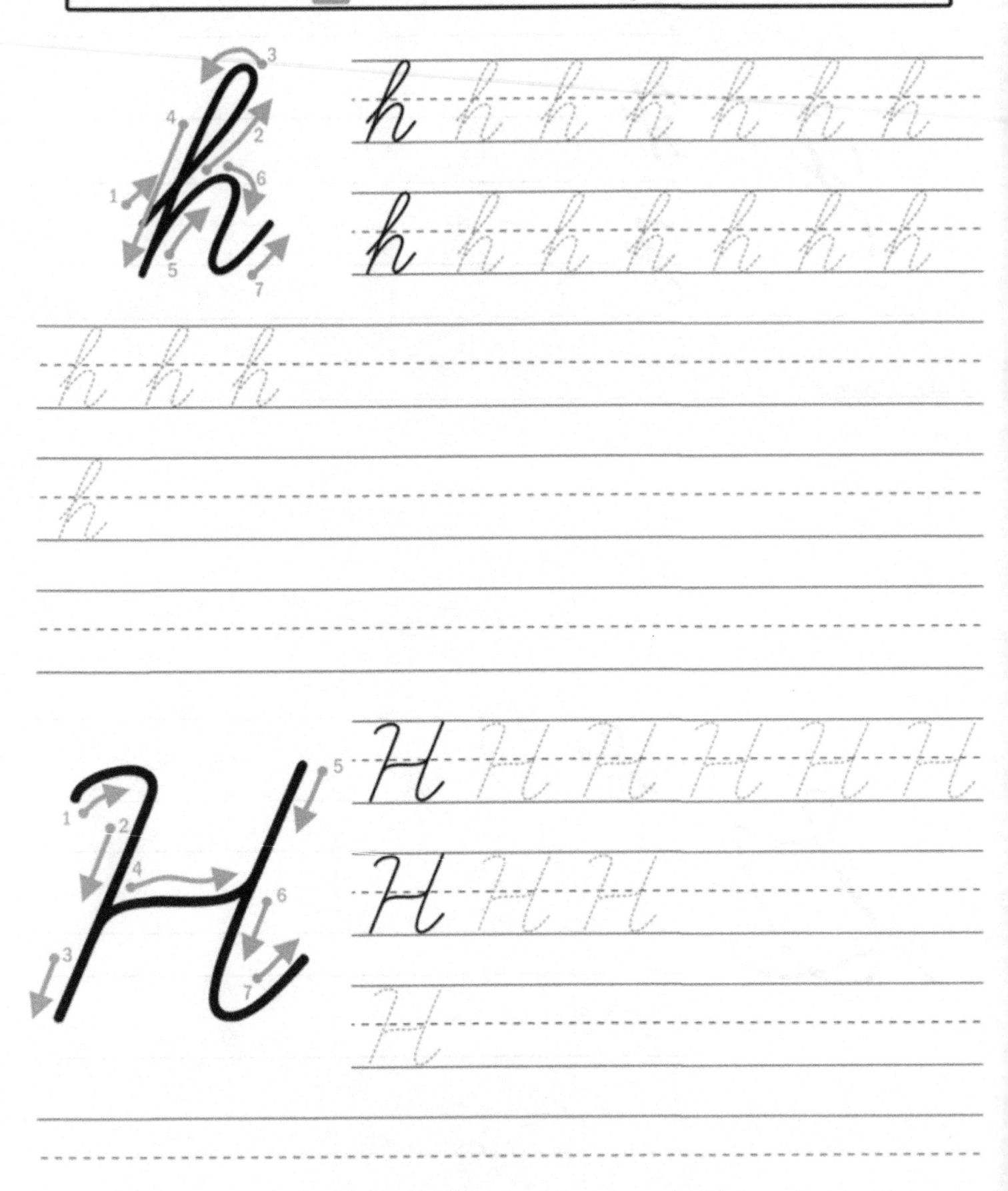

ABCDEFG**H**IJKLMNOPQRSTUVWXYZ

A B C D E F G H I J K L M N O P Q R S T U V W X Y Z

i

i

i

l

l

l

ABCDEFGHI**J**KLMNOPQRSTUVWXYZ

A B C D E F G H I J **K** L M N O P Q R S T U V W X Y Z

ABCDEFGHIJK**L**MNOPQRSTUVWXYZ

A B C D E F G H I J K L M N O P Q R S T U V W X Y Z

m *m* *m* *m* *m*

m *m* *m* *m* *m*

m *m* *m*

m

M *M* *M* *M* *M*

M *M* *M*

M

ABCDEFGHIJKLM N OPQRSTUVWXYZ

24

A B C D E F G H I J K L M N **O** P Q R S T U V W X Y Z

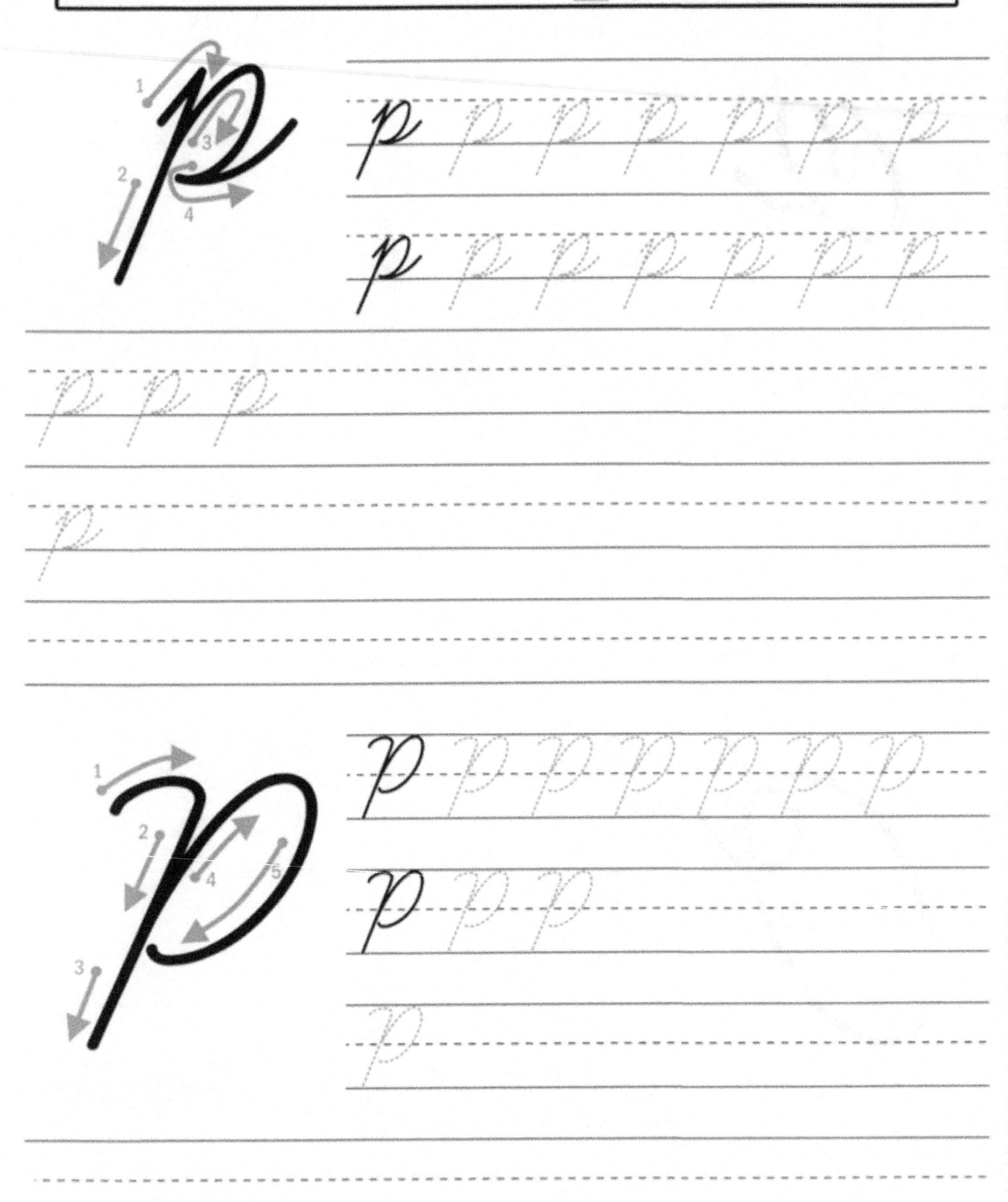

ABCDEFGHIJKLMNOPQRSTUVWXYZ

26

ABCDEFGHIJKLMNOP**Q**RSTUVWXYZ

ABCDEFGHIJKLMNOPQRSTUVWXYZ

28

A B C D E F G H I J K L M N O P Q R S T U V W X Y Z

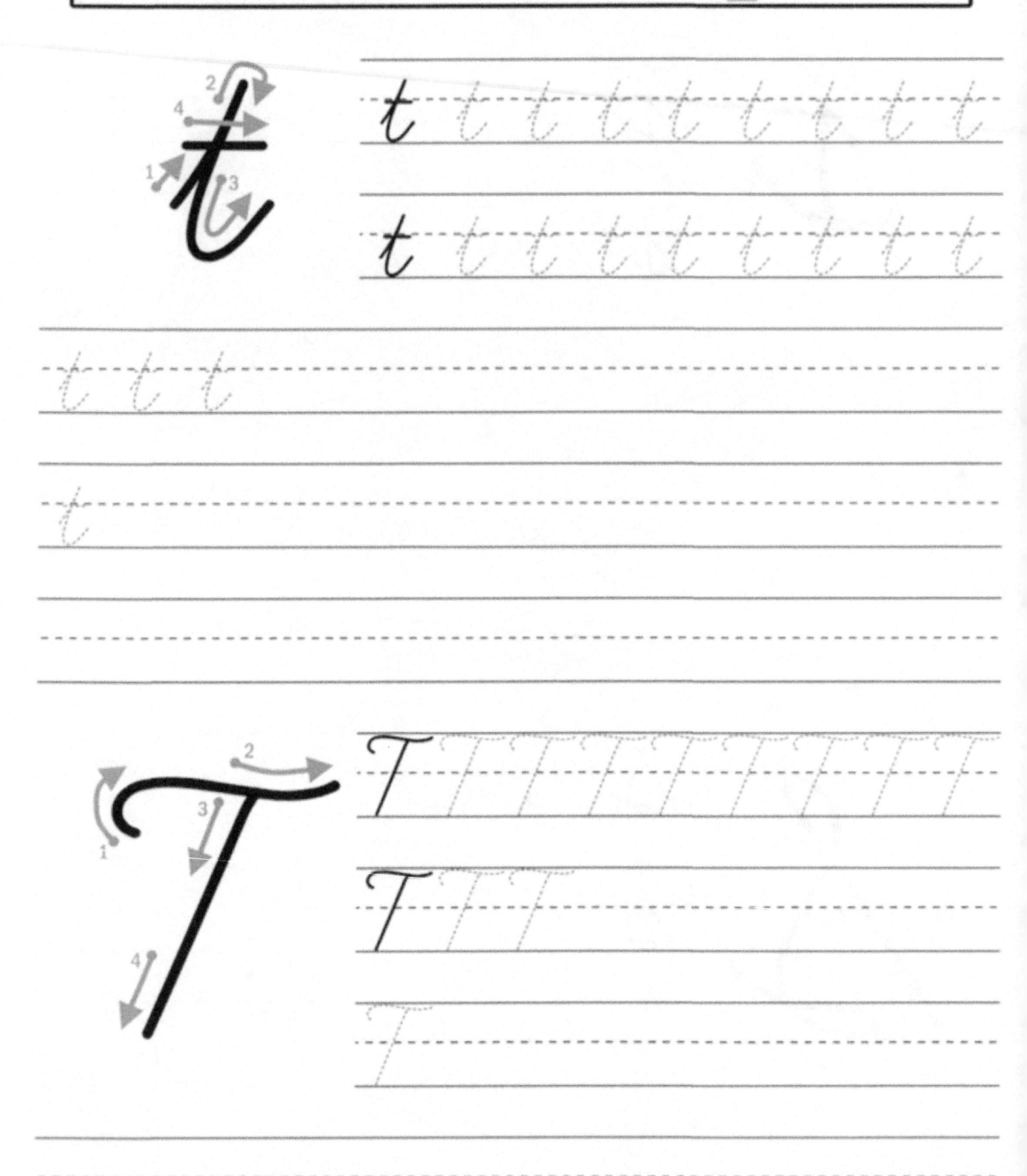

ABCDEFGHIJKLMNOPQRS**T**UVWXYZ

ABCDEFGHIJKLMNOPQRST**U**VWXYZ

ABCDEFGHIJKLMNOPQRST U V WXYZ

ABCDEFGHIJKLMNOPQRSTU**W**XYZ

ABCDEFGHIJKLMNOPQRSTUVW**X**YZ

A B C D E F G H I J K L M N O P Q R S T U V W X Y Z

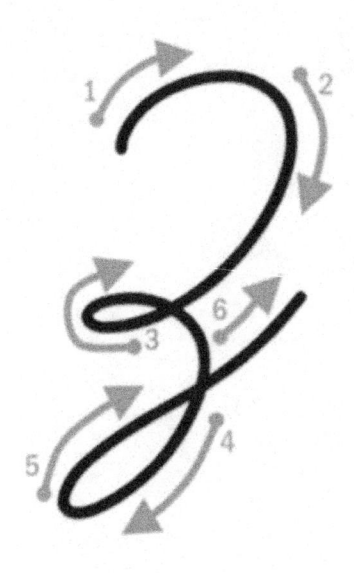

A B C D E F G H I J K L M N O P Q R S T U V W X Y Z

How to write cursive *z* (small):

How to write cursive *Z* (capital):

ABCDEFGHIJKLMNOPQRSTUVWXYZ

CURSIVE LETTERS JOINS
WORK SHEETS

ah

cd

ef

gh

gh gh gh gh

gh gh gh gh

gh gh gh gh

gh gh gh gh

ij

kl

44

op

qr

st

49

u v x

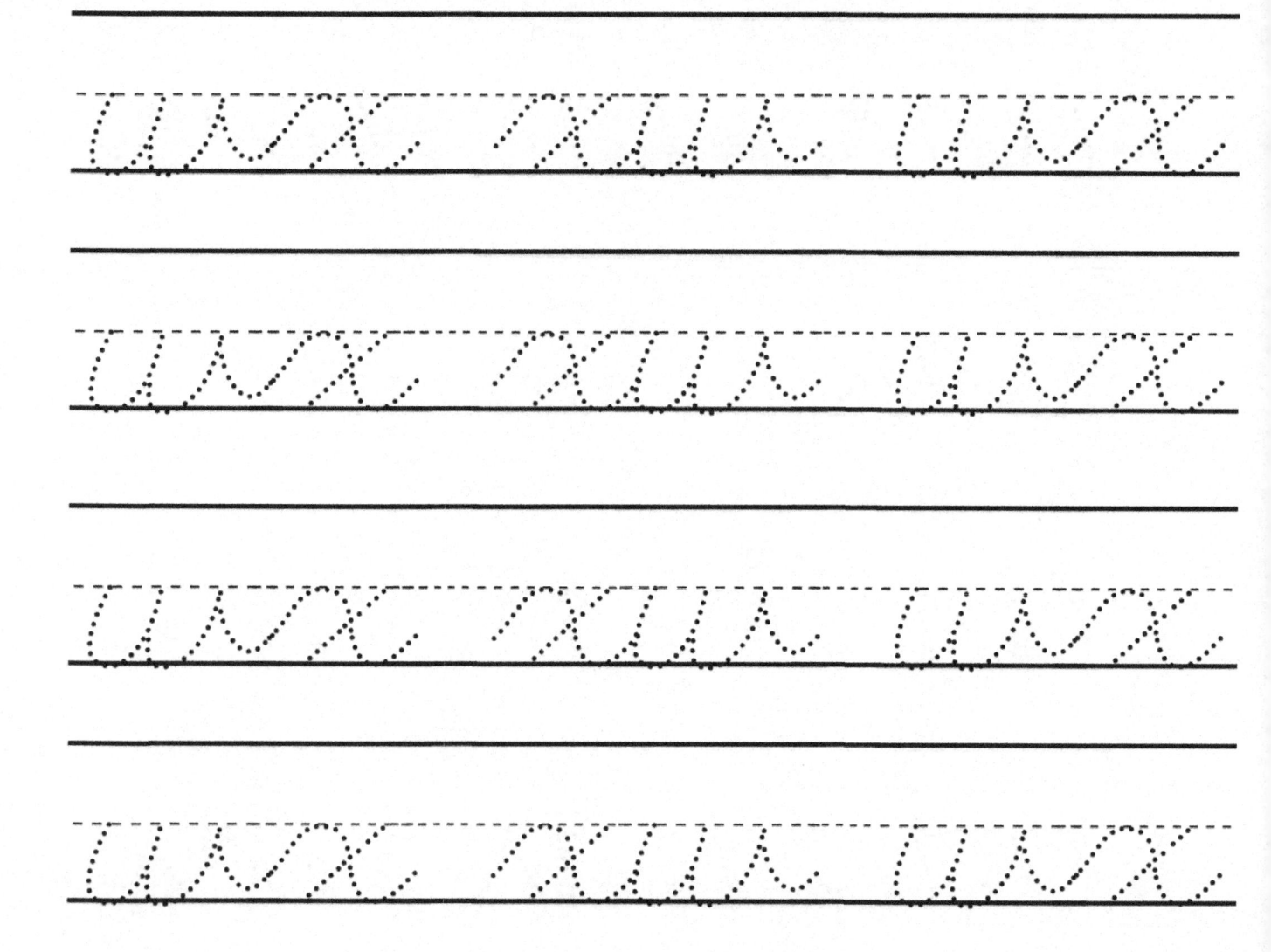

yz

yz yz yz

yz yz yz

yz yz yz

yz yz yz

Apple

CURSIVE WORDS
WORK SHEETS

Apple

Apple Apple

Apple Apple

Apple Apple

Banana

Banana

Banana

Banana

Cat

Cat Cat Cat

Cat Cat Cat

Cat Cat Cat

Dolphin

Dolphin

Dolphin

Dolphin

Egg

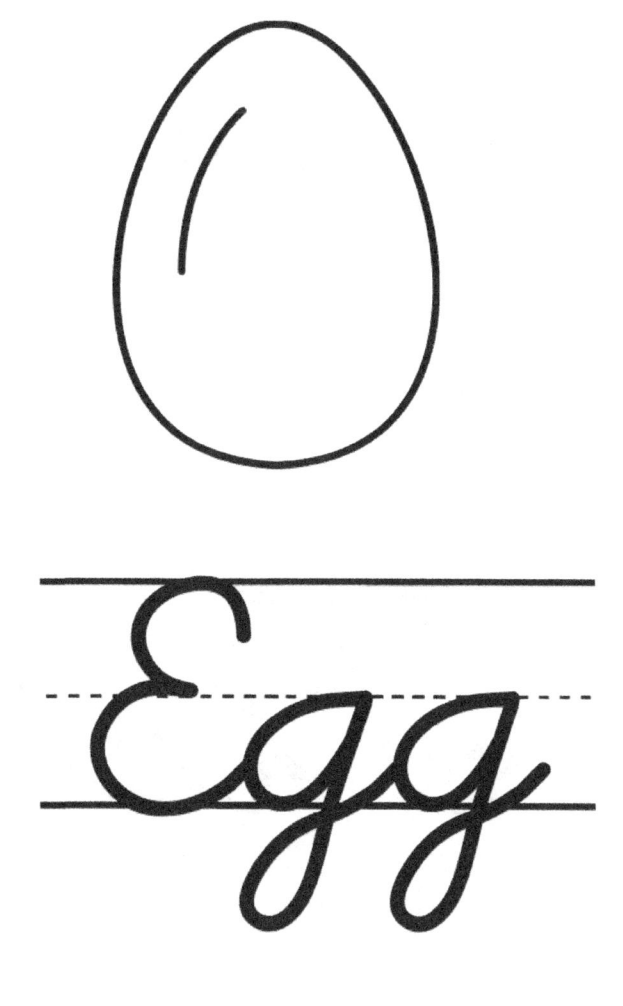

Fish

Fish Fish Fish

Fish Fish Fish

Fish Fish Fish

Guitar

Guitar

Guitar

Guitar

Home

Home Home

Home Home

Home Home

Igloo

Jar

Kite

Lion

Lion Lion

Lion Lion

Lion Lion

Mango

Mango

Mango

Mango

Nose

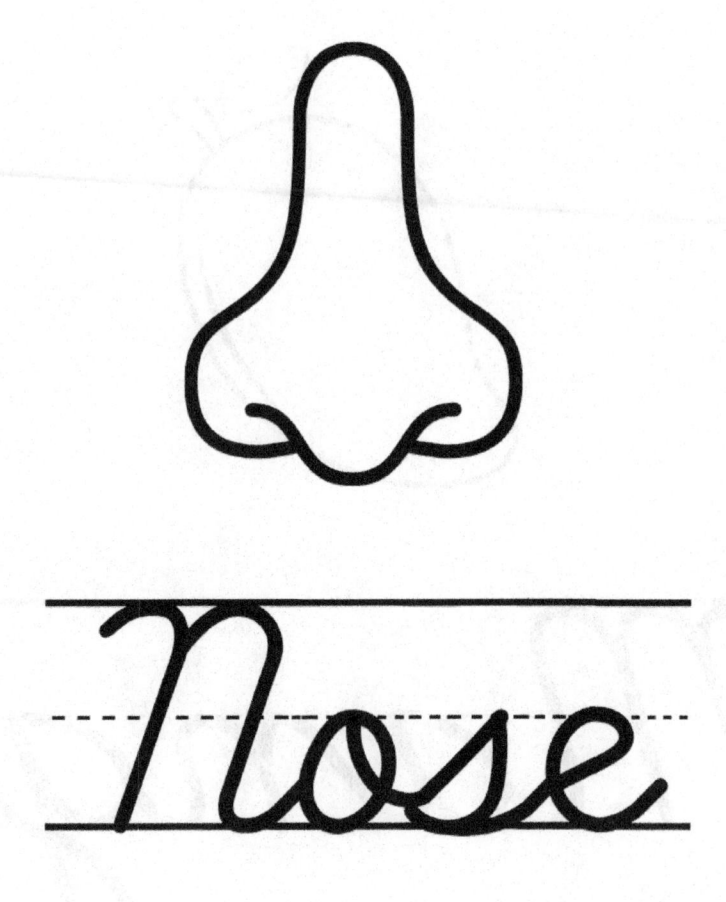

Nose Nose

Nose Nose

Nose Nose

Owl

Owl Owl

Owl Owl

Owl Owl

Pencil

Pencil

Pencil

Pencil

Queen

Queen

Queen

Queen

Rabbit

Rabbit

Rabbit

Rabbit

Sun

Sun Sun

Sun Sun

Sun Sun

Tie

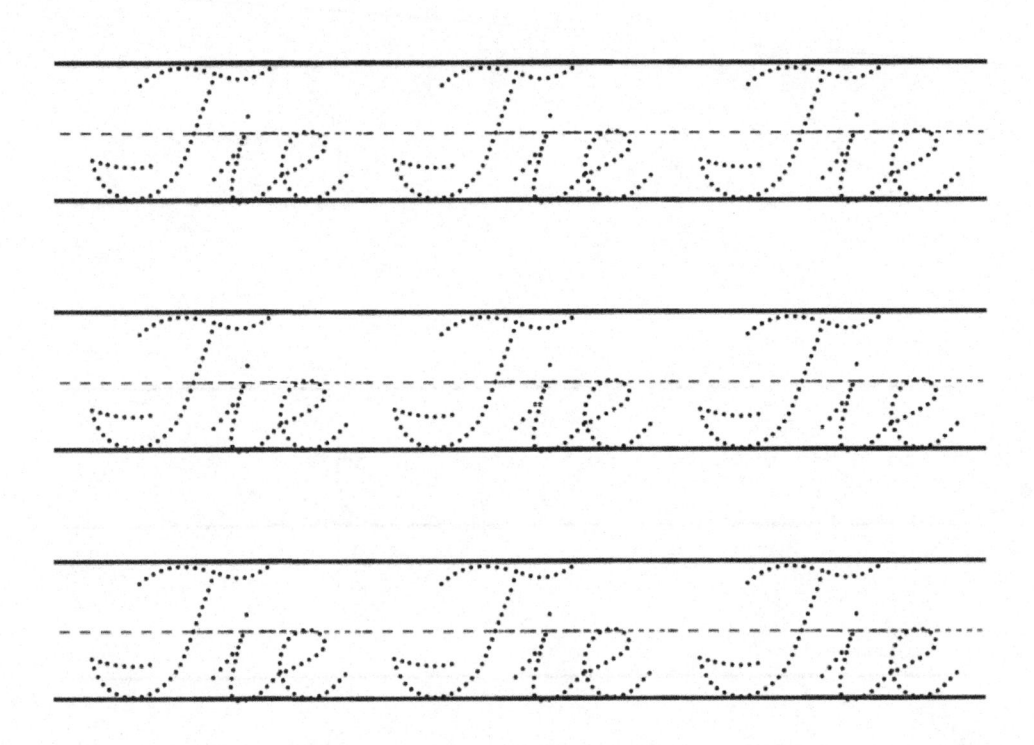

Tie Tie Tie

Tie Tie Tie

Tie Tie Tie

Unicorn

Unicorn

Unicorn

Unicorn

Van

Van Van Van

Van Van Van

Van Van Van

Whale

Whale Whale

Whale Whale

Whale Whale

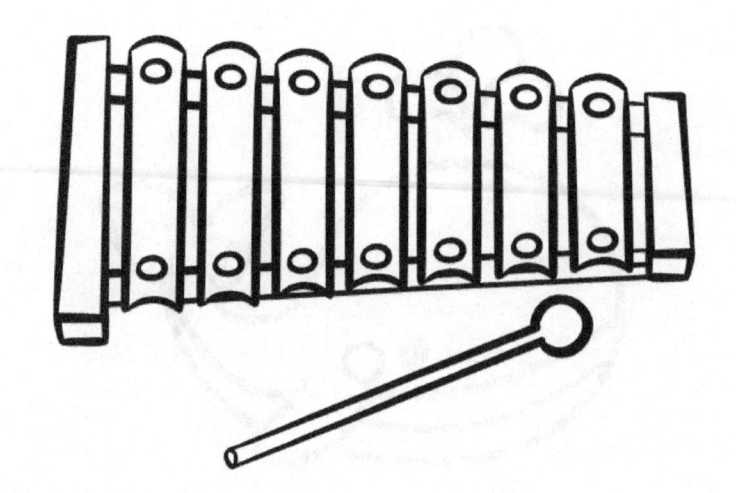

Xylophone

Xylophone

Xylophone

Xylophone

Yacht

Yacht *Yacht*

Yacht *Yacht*

Yacht *Yacht*

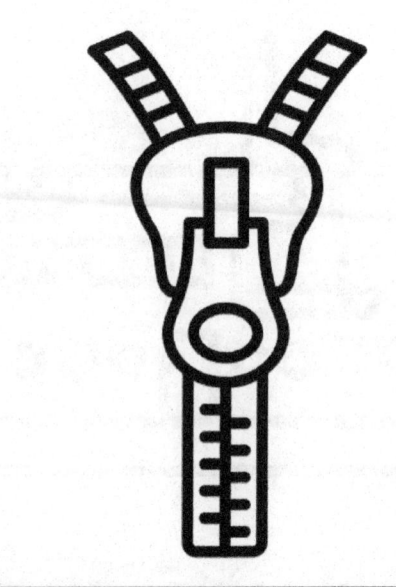

Zipper

CURSIVE
RIDDLES & JOKES
WORK SHEETS

Inscribe your answer in cursive grace, to unravel the riddle's embrace

What do you call a bear with no teeth?

A gummy bear!

What do you call a cow with no legs?

Ground beef!

Inscribe your answer in cursive grace, to unravel the riddle's embrace

What do you call an alligator in a vest?

An investigator!

Why does the math book look so sad?

Because it has many problems!

Inscribe your answer in cursive grace, to unravel the riddle's embrace

Why do sharks swim in saltwater?

Because pepper water makes them sneeze

What is brown and sticky?

A stick!

Inscribe your answer in cursive grace, to unravel the riddle's embrace

What has hands but can't clap?

A clock!

What falls in winter but never gets hurt?

The snow!

Inscribe your answer in cursive grace, to unravel the riddle's embrace

What kind of room doesn't have doors?

A mushroom!

How can you tell if someone is a good farmer?

He is outstanding in his field!

Inscribe your answer in cursive grace, to unravel the riddle's embrace

What kind of lion doesn't roar?

A dandelion!

What is brown, hairy, and wears sunglasses?

A cool coconut!

Inscribe your answer in cursive grace, to unravel the riddle's embrace

What gets wetter the more it dries?

A towel.

What has to be broken before you can use it?

An egg.

Inscribe your answer in cursive grace, to unravel the riddle's embrace

What belongs to you but is used more by others?

Your name

I'm full of keys but I can't open any door. What am I?

A piano.

Inscribe your answer in cursive grace, to unravel the riddle's embrace

What has a thumb and four fingers but is not alive?

A glove.

What kind of coat can only be put on when wet?

A coat of paint

Inscribe your answer in cursive grace, to unravel the riddle's embrace

What gets sharper the more you use it?

Your brain.

What word is spelled wrong in every dictionary?

The word "wrong!"

Inscribe your answer in cursive grace, to unravel the riddle's embrace

What is easy to get into, but hard to get out of?

Trouble!

What building has thousands of stories?

The library!

Inscribe your answer in cursive grace, to unravel the riddle's embrace

What allows you to look right through a wall?

A window!

The more you take, the more you leave behind?

What are they? Footprints!

Inscribe your answer in cursive grace, to unravel the riddle's embrace

What do dogs have that no other animal has?

Puppies!

Give me food, and I will live. Give me water, and I will die. What am I?

Fire!

Inscribe your answer in cursive grace, to unravel the riddle's embrace

What did the banana say to the dog?

Bananas can't talk.

Where do polar bears vote?

The North Poll

Inscribe your answer in cursive grace, to unravel the riddle's embrace

Why did the snake cross the road?

To get to the other side.

What did the ocean say to the pirate?

Nothing, it just waved.

Inscribe your answer in cursive grace, to unravel the riddle's embrace

What song does a cat like best?

Three Blind Mice.

What kind of kitten works for the Red Cross?

A first-aid kit.

Inscribe your answer in cursive grace, to unravel the riddle's embrace

What's a cat's favorite magazine?

A cat-alogue.

What do cats look for in a significant other?

A great purrsonality.

Inscribe your answer in cursive grace, to unravel the riddle's embrace

Why do cats hate laptops?

They don't have a mouse.

Which day of the week do cats love the most?

Caturday.

Inscribe your answer in cursive grace, to unravel the riddle's embrace

Where do cats enjoy spending a family day?

The mew-seum

What is a monster's favorite dessert?

I scream.

Inscribe your answer in cursive grace, to unravel the riddle's embrace

What room does a ghost not need?

A living room.

What do birds say on Halloween?

Trick or tweet.

Inscribe your answer in cursive grace, to unravel the riddle's embrace

Why did the zombie skip school?

He was feeling rotten.

Why didn't the skeleton go to the dance?

Because he had no body to go with.

Inscribe your answer in cursive grace, to unravel the riddle's embrace

What's a witch's favorite subject in school?

Spelling.

What do you call a witch who goes to the beach?

A sand-witch.

Inscribe your answer in cursive grace, to unravel the riddle's embrace

Where does Christmas come before Thanksgiving?

In the dictionary.

What do snowmen eat for breakfast?

Frosted Flakes.

Made in the USA
Las Vegas, NV
18 April 2024